I0188377

E IS FOR EGYPT!

E
IS FOR
EGYPT!

AUTHOR
LATOYA BEATTY

B & G Publishing

'VE BEEN COUNTING DOWN THE DAYS SINCE MY LAST BIG ADVENTURE. I JUST COULDN'T WAIT TO GET THROUGH THAT LONG, COLD WINTER!

I HAD LOTS OF TIME TO THINK ABOUT WHERE I WANTED TO GO NEXT. I PICKED SUCH A WONDERFUL, AMAZING PLACE! IT'S ONE OF THE VERY BEST!

EGYPT IS WHERE I'M GOING! THERE'LL BE LOTS OF AMAZING THINGS!

I KNOW THIS TRIP TO EGYPT IS GOING TO BE LIKE A DREAM!

NILE RIVER

GETTING TO EGYPT WAS A VERY LONG FLIGHT. IT WAS DAYTIME WHEN I LEFT, BUT WHEN I GOT THERE IT WAS NIGHT!

I FLEW OVER THE NILE RIVER. IT'S THE LONGEST RIVER IN THE WORLD! IT WAS COOL TO SEE THE SAHARA, THE LARGEST HOT DESERT IN THE WORLD!

Sahara Desert

There are lots of pyramids in Egypt! They're all beautiful and grand! Can you believe they were all made with someone's bare hands!

The largest Egyptian pyramid is the Pyramid of Khufu. It is the oldest of the seven wonders of the world! Who would've knew!

Most of the Egyptian pyramids were made as tombs for pharaohs. The most famous Egyptian pyramids are outside the city of Cairo!

Pyramids

Pharaoh

CAIRO
— EGYPT —

I WANTED TO SEE THE GREAT SPHINX OF GIZA. IT'S ONE OF THE LARGEST STATUES IN THE WORLD!

IT'S ALSO ONE OF EGYPTS MOST FAMOUS LANDMARKS! I COULDN'T MISS THAT FOR THE WORLD!

THE EGYPTIANS HAD THEIR OWN ALPHABET! THEY'RE WRITTEN WITH HIEROGLYPHS!

WHEN YOU LOOK AT OUR ALPHABET NEXT TO THEIRS, IT'S VERY VERY DIFFERENT!

THE EGYPTIAN ALPHABET HAS MORE THAN 700 HIEROGLYPHS! THATS A LOT MORE THAN 26 ENGLISH LETTERS IN THE U.S. ALPHABET!

I SAW PYRAMIDS, THE GREAT SPHINX OF GIZA, AND LEARNED ABOUT HIEROGLYPHICS. ALL THE THINGS I LEARNED WERE SO SO VERY DIFFERENT.

WHEN I THOUGHT MY ADVENTURE WAS OVER, I DISCOVERED THERE WERE MORE AMAZING THINGS! EGYPT IS WHERE MUMMIFICATION BEGAN, AND THE EGYPTIANS BELIEVED IN MORE THAN 2,000 DEITIES!

Hieroglyphs

13

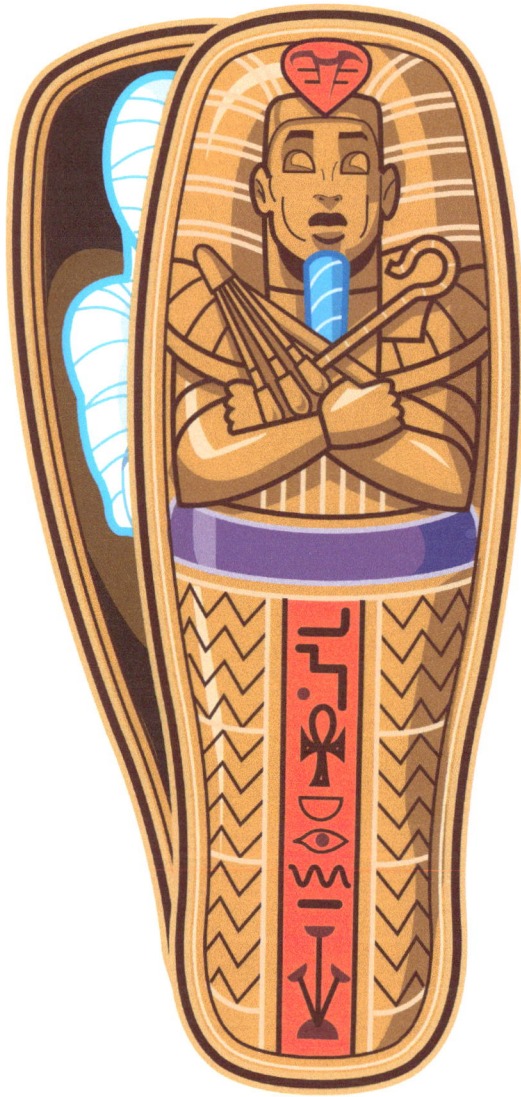

EGYPTIAN MUMMY

EGYPTIAN DEITIES

CAMEL

LONG EARED HEDGEHOG

CAPE HYRAX

WHILE IN EGYPT I SAW LOTS OF COOL ANIMALS! I SAW THE CAPE HYRAX, THE LONG-EARED HEDGEHOG, AND I EVEN RODE A CAMEL!

THERE WAS ANOTHER BEAUTIFUL SITE I HAD TO SEE BEFORE MY ADVENTURE WAS OVER. I COULDN'T LEAVE EGYPT BEFORE SEEING THE EGYPTIAN LOTUS!

EGYPTIAN LOTUS

VISITING EGYPT WAS LIKE NO OTHER ADVENTURE I'VE BEEN ON,
I CAN'T WAIT TO SEE WHERE ILL BE GOING FOR MY NEXT ONE!

I LEARNED LOTS OF NEW THINGS AND HAD GREAT FUN,
I'LL SEE YOU ON MY NEXT BIG ADVENTURE! I'VE GOT TO RUN!

EGYPT

WAIT!

WE CAN'T FORGET ABOUT THE GREAT QUEEN NEFERTITI!

NEFERTITI WAS AN EGYPTIAN QUEEN AND GREAT ROYAL WIFE OF AKHENATEN, AN EGYPTIAN PHARAOH. NEFERTITI AND THE PHARAOH PLAYED A VERY BIG ROLE IN ESTABLISHING THE ATEN CULT. THE ATEN CULT WAS A RELIGIOUS BELIEF THAT DEFINED ATEN, THE SUN, AS THE MOST IMPORTANT GOD AND THE ONLY GOD WORTHY OF WORSHIP.

NEFERTITI ABANDONED THE RELIGION OF ATEN AND WAS BANISHED BY HER HUSBAND AKHENATEN. SHE CONTINUED TO RULE UNDER THE NAME SMENKHKARE UNTIL HER STEP-SON, TUTANKHAMUN, WAS OLD ENOUGH TO TAKE THE THRONE.

LET'S LEARN THE MEANING OF SOME OF THE BIG WORDS YOU'VE READ!

PHARAOH- A RULER IN ANCIENT EGYPT.

HIEROGLYPHS- A STYLIZED PICTURE OF AN OBJECT REPRESENTING A WORD, SYLLABLE, OR SOUND.

DEITIES- A GOD OR GODDESS.

MUMMIFICATION- A PROCESS IN WHICH THE SKIN AND FLESH OF A PERSON THAT HAS DIED CAN BE PRESERVED.

KHUFU- AN ANCIENT EGYPTIAN PHARAOH THAT ORDERED THE GREAT PYRAMID OF GIZA TO BE BUILT.

LET'S SEE WHAT YOU'VE LEARNED!

WHAT RIVER IS THIS?

WHAT DESERT IS THIS?

WHAT PYRAMID IS THIS (THE BIGGEST ONE)?

_____

WHAT IS THIS CALLED?

WHAT ARE THESE?

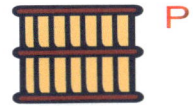

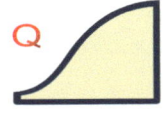

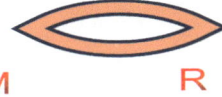

A

E

K

P

U

L

Q

V

G

B

M

R

Y

H

C

S

X

D

I

N

T

Z

CH

F

J

O

U
W

KH

WHAT ARE THESE?

WHAT ANIMAL IS THIS?

WHAT'S THE NAME OF THIS PLANT?

WHAT ANIMAL IS THIS?

_____

WHAT IS THIS ANIMAL CALLED?

GREAT JOB!

FOR JAYDEN, DJ, PRINCESS, PJ, RJ, CAELYN, NADIA, AUSTIN, AND ILLIANA.

FOR ALL THE WONDERFUL CHILDREN AT
LITTLE PANDAS CHILD CARE CENTER

IN MARTINSBURG, WV
WWW.PANDASCHILDCARE.COM

www.ingramcontent.com/pod-product-compliance
Lightning Source LLC
Chambersburg PA
CBHW040404100426

42811CB00017B/1832